HOLY INSURGENCY

Mary Biddinger

Black Lawrence Press

Black Lawrence Press
www.blacklawrence.com

Executive Editor: Diane Goettel
Book Design: Rebecca Maslen
Cover Art: "Untitled" by David Oster

ISBN: 978-1-937854-20-1

Black Lawrence Press
326 Bigham Street
Pittsburgh, PA 15211
U.S.A.

Published 2013 by Black Lawrence Press, an imprint of Dzanc Books
Printed in the United States

For the brave.

CONTENTS

I. *Anno Domini*

II. *Ave Verum Corpus*

I.

Anno Domini

DYES AND STITCHERY

I flipped out of my grandmother's hammock
and landed between stones the first time
I saw you. But you were just a sprig of asphodel

then. Seven-year-olds could buy cigarettes.
Dogs were trusted behind the wheel of a Jeep
when the owner was adequately drunk.

We had the simple things, like Crown Royal
bags for our marbles. Someone had cut
my hair with lobster scissors. I'm not even sure

if my eyes were this same color, or who was
driving me to Pike's Peak. Were you born
in a field, next to a barrel filled with burning

plywood? I imagine you walking out
of the sea instead, except we only had lakes.
They would find you clinging to a lighthouse

at midnight. There could be no other
explanation. You were destined to hotrod
a 1965 Mustang GT350 on a dirt road

with elbow-high corn on either side. You
were born to step into a pawn shop and rip
all of the guitars off the wall. Streetlights

wouldn't dare blink out when you walked by.
I had dreams of becoming a Carmelite
nun, spending every day with my onionskin

dyes and stitchery. You learned to ride
an appaloosa when your great-grandfather
abandoned you in a snowy field.

I learned to ride my first horse before
I was even alive. I knew there would be one
man courageous enough not to drink

margaritas from plastic sombreros, who
wouldn't bring a Bensenville Lolita
to the junior prom, or build his own boat

with a garbage bag sail. The day you were
born, jackhammers refused to pummel
the asphalt. There was a ghost cavern

in the center of every loaf of bread.
Bells had no more reasons not to ring.
What was once upstream traveled down.

COLLECTIONS

It was only me on a borrowed dirt bike
outside the gas station, impatient for you

to be born. In the meantime shoplifting
every new glass tumbler they issued.

Sometimes I would make a fist and slip
my entire hand inside. It looked like

a specimen. The clerk would apprehend
a teenager for abusing the dairy case,

pinching the bologna, whatever it took.
I have always been in favor of fumes.

Inhaling them as my mother filled
the tank of her Galaxie station wagon.

Imagining the way we'd burn through
the rubber mat in back, with time

and repetition. I thought I would meet
you in the center of a ring of lions.

Underwater, as two bodies weighted
and bubbling. Or even through bars,

your love letters impassioned, not
scented with rolled cloves and beer.

Who knew we would both stumble
upon the great apparition: wet grackle

ransacking half a lemon pound cake
left in the middle of the sidewalk.

We watched it for a few seconds,
without watching. My hand closed

around your fingers. I planted two
crumbs at the base of an arborvitae.

One for the clouds that gave their
blessing. One for the eye of the bird.

TREATY LINE

There were wonders, but we didn't know
they were wonders, or that they belonged

to us. The watermelon we tethered in a maple
with fishing line, just to see who would look up.

A dare involving teeth. Sentences we'd write
to burn. I traded my fear of matches for a love

of shattered plates, a restaurant where I smashed
saucers one by one before I quit. I took the apron

with me. There were children in the dust outside
the door, and I became one of them. I still have

two sides. A lake behind the house, and behind
the lake, a field. Split rails banked by chain

link. I found a place where they converge.
Here, let me put your hand on the seam.

There's a filament inside both of us, though
we never noticed. It's imaginary most days.

A man once snipped two invisible hairs
from my arm, kept them in a wooden box.

I could light that box on fire with my tongue.
It's a good thing that I didn't care. This apron

is the only one for me, its tender bleach line
at the waist. My first day, Pam laced me up.

They docked three minutes from my pay,
but now I can wear it as tight as you like.

Sometimes the trees rearrange themselves.
Everything I own I place within your reach.

CRAFTSMAN

The Northern Lights were never enough.
Storefronts all cloaked with the same
mirrored plastic. You pressed your mouth
against my neck every time we passed
the pile of bricks at the end of the street.
Now I can't bash in my own windshield
without help. I wanted to write something
on your hand, but couldn't pick a side.
There was a ghost that revealed itself to us.
After twelve we stopped counting. A little
clog of smoke in the corner of the room.
If the house was a bungalow I'd take off
my shirt the minute I walked indoors.
If the mailbox was bricked in I'd lick it
then think about starting a brush fire.
You said the only thing more beautiful
was the headless core of a deer you once
tripped over on the side of the highway.
I thought of all the abandoned fruit stands
I'd like to occupy with you on a winter day.
We would find the heap of twine forgotten
after the pumpkins were gone. They never
build fruit stands out of brick, just boards.
Lumber left when your father ripped down
the addition he hammered drunk one night.
He said he was building you a bedroom.
You told him it was twenty years too late.
If only you could hold the entire town
in your right hand. The bobcat in bed
with the wren. The wren small enough
to wear in a holster against my body.
I'd spend all day waiting for it to move.

ODE TO YOUR INNOCENCE

Your innocence was the demon-eyed pony
at the edge of the carousel. Its saddle always
damp, like a harmonica. The only one I would
ever ride. The only one with an open mouth.

The bus departed at 4:15. A storm bent trees
to the ground. I couldn't circle the block.
Jammed between the trash can and a pair
of binoculars: your innocence, left out
like a glove that never fit a wire rack.

I have pressed myself against many men.
In the blank hallways of the hospital, slipped
my hands into pockets that weren't mine.
A rapid infuser no match for your innocence.

At first I didn't know that your innocence
was innocence, but it was always yours.
I didn't know what to call it, tried *majesty*,
hypomania. Attempted divining you
from an old well filled with handkerchiefs.

I had your innocence all afternoon. After
the afternoon I had your innocence again.
It wasn't like a vinyl smock at all. Oh
no, it was the exact opposite of that.

I was born precocious. Walked right out
of my mother's arms, and into the tavern.
All the men there had wives, and cameras.
My innocence was a rice paper balloon.

When did I lose interest in everything else?
Didn't want to shake hands with the gold
medalist, or take photographs of newly-
hatched doves. I thought you were a ghost.
Tried to scream into the bubbling springs.
Your innocence became my only food.

A man said something about the speed
of sound. We'd be chasing it forever,
he claimed. Like your innocence, slipped
to me under a table, and the ten seconds
it would take to warm it in my hand.

Some men walk through their women.
I held you still. Your innocence wrapped
around us like electrical tape. We left
the lights on. The refrigerator hummed
its song about a bad journey to Memphis.
There wasn't anything left to believe.

HERESY

Around this time I stopped
believing. I wanted to drown

all of the wreaths in the river.
Even the one with a cornsilk

rabbit. Especially the eggs,
the way they mocked us all

April. I was a cat walking
across a stove. My winter

coat became a strangler.
Only you could help me

out of it. How many books
could I stack in one paper

bag before the bottom tore?
The answer had something

to do with your arms, but I
never asked you to carry it.

Every day I would peel one
strip of vinyl siding off my

house. I started at the back.
There was shimmery tar

on damp wood underneath.
I did the same thing with

myself and called it purpose.
There was nothing to hate

more than the moon, lone
saucepan of simmering rice.

You wanted an archipelago
so we made one. Walking

down my street near dawn,
I could count all the houses

where someone was awake,
carnation of a lamp behind

old drapes. I wanted to press
my hand against your chest.

The four your body made
under sheets, one leg bent.

I would burn hydrangeas
in a metal drum all night.

A GAUNTLET

They thought the triple beam
would trick me, the cow bell lure me
into a field woven with artificial corn.

But no thank you, calm waters.
I've had more than my share
of the eels underneath, even if edible

in some other country. The country
we made of our bodies flipped
the census into hyperion mode.

Nobody knew the combination.
We wouldn't tell. In our next life
we would decline a next life

the same way we refused the spoon
with a wasp hidden underneath.
Your mouth was a force of creation.

It always knew the whereabouts
of its double. They made us watch
a short film about the genesis

of utilitarianism. The storms
were real storms, and the plagues
quite believable. Before the roof

roiled with magnetized staples,
you stripped off my chainmail bra.
I couldn't call this unpredictable

but I was nonetheless thankful,
vowed to dismantle any twine
codpiece they might try to install.

When they tied us to a tree
we linked arms until it dissolved
into a straw of sap. Even though

you were a man, you learned how
to weave me a pair of elbow-length
gloves. The detailing exquisite.

You asked how many days
until we could, as they say, *throw
down*. But we were born fighting.

Not each other, just the chill
at the bottom of the filmy lagoon.
The forces that weren't really

forces, just hulking stalactites
clustered at the cave door,
waiting for the drop of your fist.

PRELUDE TO OUR ESCAPE

They'd pile bricks all over us,
or invent an ocean, then merge
the ocean with another ocean
to make it vaster. More space
for jellyfish and eels. But no.
It will still be us in the elevator,
some man with a high collar
eyeing me as I slide my hands
into your coat. Outside: hail
the size of quinces, bouncing
on the lawn. They'd chain me
to the sewer grate and release
the angriest owl. I once wrote
an entire book on penetration,
but that research would be moot
in a room crossed by red lasers.
Thankfully I can walk without
making a sound. The only noise:
the tap of my necklace as it hits
my bottom lip in rhythm with
rain. If I could always look out
your windows I would promise
not to throw rocks. How could I,
when your cheekbone settles
into the exact dip of my palm?
The first time it happened in bed.
There were swords suspended
above us, from sugar twine ropes.
I pressed my hand into anything
that would take. Held the bread
dough up to my temple as a test.
They'd cut things out of me.
Chase me down the street with

torches. Tie us back to back
above the vat. It's a good thing
that I know how to cook. No
match for when wolves stream
out of the hills, brushing soft
against our arms. The knives
we had no idea we'd ever find.

SIMPLICITY PATTERN #2519

Behold the corridor of Woodward Avenue
in front of me, sad ladies in the dress shop
windows, waiting to shrug out of their gowns.
The way I would lean into the counter, as if
it could love me back. And they handed over
their fifties, offered me a furnished room.
They thought that I could wait it all out.
There was something quaint about my skirt.
Everyone wondered if I had made it myself.
Of course there would be matching gloves.
Cheese fondue on a hot plate, with wine
poured in grandmother's everyday globes.
An excavator busy next door, making way.
A car that miraculously fired on the third try.
And somewhere past the city park, horizon
emptied itself into highway, a gorge with no
water at the crest. The way I found a trail
into the trees. I didn't look back to watch
the car sink. Who could look past your arms,
windows with ice on both sides, my own ice
a product of surprise. They say each stone
has its own distinct ring, like every shadow
attaches itself to the moon. We all need
a stalker, if not a conjugate. Nothing but
canned light in my grotto at opening time.

METROPOLIS

In the city where you were born
snow hovers gray like chain link
and skies ignite. I stand against
your body and point to a house
where every crack is a flame.

Every flame is a house. Geese
don't even bother to fly by.
You tell me that your city
would fit into mine. Garters
wouldn't hold anything back

for long. In the city where you
were born, lights don't stay on
all night. My city walks into
a bar, and admires your city's
belt buckle. Never before such

a herald of sparks. Everyone
knows my city: slaughterhouses
and red sequins, the rivers so
still that nobody can truly break

the surface. Once we walked
over my city's rattling bridges,
the ribcage that rises from rest
and sucks air in, exhales it to
your city, which is always

ready for more. Your city
drops its change in the street
if only to watch my city
bend and pick it up. I call
this distasteful, but my city

falls for it every time.
Neither of us had wheat
fields, or squirrels to coax
indoors with buttered corn.
That's not where we hail

from. My city flags a taxi
and yours runs in the rain.
Somebody burned both
of the twin steeples years
ago, after we moved out,

and none of this matters.
There's a pile of sticks
at the edge of the freeway.
When we come to the end
of a road, there's more road.

A BILDUNGSROMAN

Begins with the two of us, like paper dolls
accidentally printed too close, and overlapping

in the most unseemly places. One coal-chute
black sweep for the hair. Hands missing

fingernails, but webbed together somehow,
albeit invisibly. Watch us lean in unison

over a thumbnail sketch of watermelon
loaded with fireworks. Certainly we could

outdo the catastrophe. There was a sandstorm.
We just stood there and laughed as people

ran for their cars. We only drove each other.
Never purchased clothing that would not

fit both of us if necessary. An unrelenting
sandstorm can tear pigtails off a copperhead,

the gunsmoke from a gunnysack. Ladyfingers
shimmied across the floor of the cafeteria

and all the women ripped their pantyhose
in anticipation. We commandeered both

microphones and I sang to you the ballad
of my haunted eyelid, the flowerpot that tried

to rival you in my affections, and how all
of this ended quite badly, except for us.

NATURALISM

We contemplated the giant pendulum
in the museum until it pummeled us,

retreated, then pummeled us again.
I landed behind the admission desk.

You lodged between two mastodons
and not happy. It took several tries

to shove my hip back into its socket.
We'd practiced informally every day,

not with so many people watching.
The docent helped me back into my

jacket, handed you a museum map.
At this point we did not expect any

sabotage of the gem gallery, loosing
of scorpions believed dead for years

but really sleeping. The only way back
was through the bat cave, source of all

claustrophobia. I slipped my arms up
the front of your shirt for comfort. Old

fears reignited like a dinosaur sponge
exploding out of a capsule to terrorize

the bathtub. I just wanted to be home.
But a pair can't spend all its days in

bed. Hours before we were feeding
each other torn shreds of deli turkey

at the edge of a retention pond. How
else to spend a Saturday? And what

was lurking at the mouth of the cave
but my fifth grade teacher, brushing

her hair with the same fierce motion
she used in the classroom to ignite

Bunsen burners. I flung my body
over you immediately, instinctively

as a black-naped tern vomited its way
to safety. I tried my best to protect

your head. The guards didn't know
us and thought it was assault, locked

me in the archives while you refused
to eat an ice cream cone. At long last

they removed the tape from my wrists.
You'd already dug a tunnel halfway

to my chamber. We found each other
down there. The night guards tossed

jelly beans at the celestial diagram,
but we did not report them. Instead

we dominated the butterfly pavilion,
taught the pendulum a new vector.

WHERE YOU STORE THE GUN AT NIGHT

There was no boundary to your acres,
just a string buried somewhere under ice.
A moon for the sake of being a moon.
I'd touch it. Wouldn't you, in the right

combination of smoke-fluster and snow?
There was once a dream about flannel
and under that flannel there was even more.
I was never good at measuring anything,

especially time. If there was a wooden box
big enough for both of us, we could hide it
on the top shelf, next to the kidskin wallet
and fingernail adhesive my grandmother

left behind. I'd never ask you to climb
onto the roof without me. Sometimes
a mattress creates its own secret space.
When I was sixteen I first discovered it:

a trail of sugar crystals on a thread.
The piece of paper that once crossed
your lips, only neither of us knew it yet.
I tucked my Sulphide marbles inside

a jacket that you never wore. Suspended
in the shooter: a fleck of a girl, and her
milk bucket. I would carry mine all day
if it kept your hands from turning red.

ROUTE 31

We both felt too close
to the sky, but who could stop

us? All of the rain changed
its mind and became mist,

or resisted naming. We had no
words, and didn't need coats.

I imagined myself as the pale
dun from your childhood,

brown stretch across highway
onto the shoulder, color of deer

hide tanned by snowfall or plow.
Same shade as the back of your

neck in June. You didn't listen
to the lady with the burlap voice.

She told you to get back in
line. I was the girl who pulled

you out by the hand, clouds
turning green overhead. Nobody

else bothered asking the trees.
Three miles away, beneath

an abandoned rowboat, first
time I pressed my hand against

your cheek. I would never
take it away. We flattened into

the soil, two switchblades out
of our handles and gleaming.

CONFABULATIONS

When the car couldn't drive on
we pushed it. We were looking
for something heavy enough
to resist us, the penumbra
we couldn't help broadcasting.
Everyone spun out except
us, but not because we were
particularly grounded.

Whenever I walked into church
you bent me back over the oak
desk in my bedroom again.
It wasn't the reaction I intended,
but I felt it. Statues shivered.
I remembered salmonella,
the way it felt when nuns
handed me two dusty erasers
and led me out the back door.

You thought biting my lip
would help, but on the lawn
I saw the bodies of two maple
twigs intersecting. A shadow
ribbon our hips made. I tried not
to leave toothmarks on your neck
but where else could I put them?
The crossing guard linked an arm
through mine and said *hold it*.

A VERY HARD TIME

The lawns were wet because
we made them that way.

A man on the television noted
difficulties, the new trouble

with air, schoolgirls loosing
their braids in directions

that could only mean evil.
Of course I wasn't watching.

My face was buried in your lap.
You weren't going anywhere.

Someone was stealing all
of the lawnmowers, rolling

them across the highway,
but you tangled your hands

in my hair. Did not consult
the shotgun. Later, in bed,

the headlights of an ancient
station wagon slashed across

my body, like a reverse fever.
Its radio blasted ragtime.

Nobody could afford feathers
anymore. I performed my fan

dance with folded paper towels.
You never minded, and we

always found use for them.
It was all about utility.

The incident in the stairwell
had solidified our contract.

It helped that we never
ate anything but each other.

CONFLUENCE

In place of everything that came
before: the soldier until he died
a soldier's death, ordinary and quick.

A woman traveling east on a train.
Seven boxes tied shut with string.
Ground that refused to be anything

but ground. How many years did they
occupy the space we now inhabit,
the things we wished we'd invented

but knew better? When I first saw
you I became the lesser of two
steeples, neither of them with bells.

I held your shoulder square in my
hand, and miles away a grouse fell
straight from an oak into flame.

You fished my hat out of the river,
so I threw it back, if only to glimpse
the translucence of your shirtsleeves.

We ran through pine woods every
night. I scrawled lines on birch bark
and buried them at your feet as you

pretended to scowl. We counted
the number of ways that we could
pin ourselves together. The soldier

left no shadows in our bedroom.
They'd shipped him back twenty
years before, solemn in a flag box.

The woman waited at the station
eating lemon ice. One hand raised
to block the sun, the train a fly

stapled at the edge of a cornfield.
I would claim that I have her eyes,
but those were lost to the Pacific.

Countless fish surrounded her face
like crinoline, then scattered at once.
Clouded water all they left behind.

I felt her when thunderheads dipped
past the ridgeline, or if you startled
in sleep and couldn't find the light.

I dropped a glass that crashed into
the sidewalk. Instead of sweeping
up pieces, you carried me away

to the hill where they once stood.
She lowered the brim of her hat.
He scanned steeple tops for rain.

DOCUMENTARY ON THE DEATH
OF A SMALL BIRD

You said *there is no such thing as a common wren.*
Something about an articulation, a hollowness

we could never experience, being warm blooded
and so in love. My friend once presented a bloated

Canada goose to his mother, replete with worms.
She refused to make sausage. The hysterics ensued

until a neighbor wrapped the goose in a silk slip.
If only more things were hydraulic, then perhaps

we would be content with the honorable mention.
We might line our roofs with down instead of tar.

I suggested we burn the wren for lack of twigs,
or truss it like a game hen, stuffed with pecans.

Your grandfather once wore a hat with a feather,
so why not tuck the wren into the nearest brim.

Nearby, two men halved an oak with a rip saw.
Not a metaphor for the merits of slow progress.

Hardly an ominous gesture to the universe, which
lapped the backs of our legs, then closed its wings.

PORTRAIT OF MYSELF AS A PIECE OF RED CANDY IN YOUR MOUTH

Dear tongue, how can anyone call you a beginning? There's only one way in. The birds of the trees remain countable. The fringe on a jacket can still hover midair. We put everything on stop, and then held it. Wherever I looked there were raspberries. I needed a new name for the sky. Tooth marks, not fruit. The sky was a tongue. No it wasn't. The tongue began with you and ended some miles over my right shoulder. Your bed was a boat we didn't mind boarding. Neither of us had to stay behind on the dock. You asked me what shape is this cloud, what sound is that you're making. I dreamed about a suitcase, and when we woke the room was a spill of silver leaves. The first thing I searched for was your tongue, not the extinguisher. Another woman would fumble for her undergarments. The woman I never was would do nothing. In some other hemisphere, a bird lives exclusively on human sweat. I would perish within moments unless buried in the crease of your neck. Somewhere a man watches a newspaper slide into a lake. You will never have to be that man.

THE BUSINESS OF IT

At a certain point I began to wonder
what the springs in the mattress thought
of us. Whether there was somebody

in there, keeping track. They'd set all
the racehorses free weeks earlier.
My body learned not to register thunder

as something beyond a disruption.
Asleep with my head on your shoulder,
it seemed fitting that the mares left

last. My own fingers demonstrated how.
You asked if it was a detonation,
or more like the euphoria of black ants

crawling one by one into a straw.
Their exodus the opposite of our bed's
migration. And what about clocks

left gutted on a sawhorse, gold entrails.
Who could trust them again, once
the gears were subjected to daylight?

No answers from the stable boy,
pitching bales into the chipper at dawn.
When they hauled our old mattress

away, they promised it would become
a haven for orphaned magpies.
Even the stitching would be unstitched

in the name of conservation. *How
dreadful*, you said. And our bed inched
across the last remaining pasture.

SAINT VODKA

The matchmaking service for geese
failed, and so did the stone wall

meant to sequester our new territory.
Nobody published dissertations

on the shameful tendencies of metals,
the way water didn't lap edges

but rather floundered, oxidizing,
or whatever was in fashion.

I was making a noise that sounded
like ouch but meant the opposite.

You were posed without donkey,
exact likeness of a medieval

saint on my grandmother's goblet.
Everything was beyond stupid.

The last marble swallowed in town
square, and nobody dared to stay

for the resurrection. We'd invent
our own elixir as anesthetic.

Tried to register ourselves for cult
status, though we were just

a pair. At the moment you arrived
I was stationed in garage sale

blankets on a Chicago sidewalk,
wondering if the moon had

a purpose. You were more lucid
than the clearest gelatin lamb

in my grandmother's refrigerator.
She'd suspend one penny

in the dead center as appendix.
I'd flip it on my tongue.

Your clarity was inexplicable.
We refused to let them

hang bells from our shoulders.
Conflated hagiographies

until all that remained was ice
and a hangnail of mirror.

A POVERTY

It wasn't a paper flower they left
at the crash site, but somebody's
underpants, dimpled with rain.

Pink, for forgiveness and speed.
Our apartment was the lost space
between a walnut's hemispheres.

Our bodies the sole inspiration
for Velcro, though we earned no
royalties, just clung all afternoon.

There was nowhere else to be.
The difficult times were upon us.
We spread them out like maps

then situated our bare selves
on top of them. Down the block,
colonials vomited their contents

onto the parkway. Box fans
must have been reproducing
in the bushes. Every house had

at least two, sometimes still
circling. One fan romanced
the leg of a dead hobbyhorse.

A shiver struck me, thinking
of our toaster oven evicted
from its den on the counter.

We broke into the abandoned
barbershop, but nobody cared.
You spun me in the chair. We

did not cut a thing. The red wig
stationed beside a mailbox never
grew on its own, or flew away.

II.

Ave Verum Corpus

A RIGID TRADITIONALIST

You wrote your ode to Jesus in eight days,
then burned your desk and never wrote again.

Untrue! You wrote your next ode just for me.
A bag half-filled with stones. No hummingbird.

We walked to Sunday concerts in the rain.
You worried Michael Bolton would steal me

and wear my golden sandals like a cross.
There was no chance he was as huge as you.

(They told me I would never dance again).
Somehow the stage dissolved into a mist,

the singer ducking underpants and bricks.
My theory promised candles, beds, and silk,

your postulate more axiom than skin.
And what of all the gates blocking our way,

wrought iron poles so pointless to the slim
who simply step between the right and left.

The mayor clapped whenever we slipped in.
Somewhere, a lake engulfed another lake.

You wrote your ode to longing, overnight.
Your endings still began where they began.

MY GOD

In order to understand
how a tree burns, try storm

when the fence of poplars
means less than skin.

Think whim, straw hats
woven too small

to fit anything that lives.
Oh, this. No, this:

a seam of tape to hold
my cardboard box

intact. They showed me
that. I ran the metal

edge along my lip.
You weren't supposed

a penitent until confessed.
Unbuttoned dress

or a black ink X.
A misleading sympathy

involving your tin
mouth, a bruise the shape

of a golden plover
standing on a rusted cliff.

You drove me from one
series of birches

to the next. No matter where
or how I pressed.

A GENESIS

I caught you gleaming. But you
invented me with your mouth.
We were *cut from the same cloth
of awesomeness*. Our glory
could stop wars. The azaleas shut
their blooms when you opened
me. A new kind of reverence
broke tabletops instead of mending.
The city sent us a letter asking
to harness our heat for infrastructure
development. How many cranes
could we power back into the sky?
There was a dead house nearby,
and only we could rock it back into
its foundation. We signed no
contract because we didn't need to.
The shutters were all hanging.
I stepped on a crisp winged ant
and you dispatched it. Water
flowed like chitchat in the cellar.
We started in the living room.
Never touched the bloated red sofa.
I had my eye to a triangular
window. Paint on its sill stopped
peeling when it saw my thigh.
You began when you saw my thigh.
My thigh could educate entire
districts. My left breast knew more
than the average philosopher.
Officials stopped by to inspect us.
Someone brought a gigantic
key, but you dwarfed it, made them
hurry back to the squad car

as if it had never happened. Next
we ransacked the attic, pink
frizz of insulation lapping at us.
We were immune to its fibers,
watched the eaves hustle westward.
At the end of the day, the day
still hadn't ended. The mayor threw
a fireworks reception, begged us
to send a golden spider into the sky.

AN INCARNATION

Sorrow? And what for?
After everything's expunged

we'll be teeth in the teapot,
throwing orange peels

at the prophet. Detail
the inches that might exist

between us, as if anything
could. I'd issue you

the most delicious
violation ever on the books

in our county. Did it really
have *a seat*? If so,

why not consult us
for infrastructure advice

before handing grenades
to the goblins?

In the woods, you
promised to show me your

doctrine. I demonstrated my
theorem. Two magpies

coupled wildly nearby.
The tree stumps all in rows,

like lockers. We defined our
genius like we ate

our way through
every resurrection in sight.

O HOLY INSURGENCY

Overthrow me. It's not hard
unless you say it is. Gone:

envelopes with nothing inside,
paprika burns on a tongue

that invents its own reverse
chronology. Nothing left

to mend, but that's not so true.
Every night we remake us

as our skin transubstantiates.
They say there's no such

wound. I once stole a book up
my shirt, ran ten blocks

before opening the cover. You
were nestled in the pages.

The newspapers moaned on
about a town in ruins.

At the time I had no belief
in my own insurrection.

I was the product of hollow
olives and damp wool.

Vowed at that moment never
to regale you with stories

of my childhood dog, or ram
my fingers through

your shimmering flan at dinner.
No such thing as harm.

I've forgotten it completely.
Every day in its place.

A PACT

After the twelfth time listening
to *Working in a Coal Mine*
at the pie counter of Uncle Rowdy's,
my powder blue sandal falling off
as if I meant it, we decided never
again. They had barely started
boarding up the window.
Thunderbird fragments daggered
the revolving cake case,
though only one red velvet died.
We didn't mind the spilled gasoline
and you kissed me. I pulled all
of the broken glass from your jacket.
You liked its sheen, but it wasn't good
for either of us. At home: two plates,
a bedspread pattern that looked like
anteaters copulating in a valley.
Grandmother called it paisley.
You called it ridiculous, but still
pulled me by my legs to the corner,
where baby anteaters sprung from
what looked like a leather hassock.
When you rolled me over, I divided
the number of claws by skulls.
Nobody had to tell us to hit the floor.
We'd developed our senses
for sport. You'd crush an egg
in your hand, and I'd write on paper
how many fragments would stick.
We'd lay our guns together
on the dresser, touching but not
overlapping. It was like the time
my hand slipped right through

a peach. Of course we didn't have
guns. We were too fast to need them.
Everyone babbling about bacteria,
the moon. All we wanted was keys.
You said you could taste the Detroit
in every angle of me. You filled
my mouth with a hundred boats
at night, all lit with paper lanterns.

A SINGULARITY

Just because it moves doesn't mean
it's alive, or so she said. But when
did she learn how to walk on her own,
or did she. No, she never did, because
there wasn't enough rain in the barrel

to hold a world more than half water.
His world was more than half water.
Sometimes there were common doves
that looked spectacular from far away.
They were those doves, so light found

its way around them in a sort of halo
that meant nothing short of holiness.
What did it mean to be holy, in a room
dominated by ceiling instead of walls.
She caught him looking up at it. No,

he never did, there were other things
more pressing, such as bodies, always
the together of them. When his hand
fell, hers rose. When he was a child
he made a man out of leaves rigged

with fishing line. Her favorite doll
was a girl on one side, and beneath
the red gingham skirt, a wolf. Neither
remembered the sound of glass on
pavement, but they embodied it.

No river sharp enough. Countless
embargos overturned with one shove.
A sweep of the hand. One day found
themselves in a forest that could not
contain them. The branch-fall. Lone

stag on a rock that wasn't a stag or
a rock, but the outline of him in rain.
And the shadow was not his but hers.
When a glass broke on the sidewalk
she was the creep toward the grass

while he pooled around fragments.
They were both field and stream.
Autumn and spring fused to one
single season where the leaves died
and reopened, and then died again.

A CORONATION

I belong in the second category,
hammered into the siding along
with all the other nails, only
this one made it clear through,
and alleluia. Now untie me
so we can parade the avenues.
The restless patients all waving
their tentacles in our direction.
We were so ready for fireworks
we hushed in the closet and lit
just a couple of them. And now
the entire neighborhood's ablaze.
I brought my hot glue gun along
since we had nothing on a leash.
The matching straw hats clearly
too much, but that didn't deter us
from passing them to strangers.
We refused to honor the street
definition of *chronic*. Youthful
defiance was best demonstrated
by my mouth's insubordination
in times of dire panic. Translated:

no measure to calculate the drift
of my lips down your back. If ships
were alive they would drive west
into the gray of an afternoon only
meant to bisect us. A ship within
a ship. Outside we found the deck
and an anchor rope. We begged to
dive in, even if the sea was green.
The only backdrop in sight: brick
and the leavening grit to pin brick

upon brick. I made just one point
that night when pressed against
the length of your body. Neither
of us asleep yet, one frog outside
waiting for a reply to its queries.
You said the trees were desperate,
or else why would they stand that
still. I told you they'd been moving
the same way for a thousand years.

FORENSICS

I once believed you were a dead man
from Memphis, and then why try

when so many flags manage to knot
themselves despite the odds.

In the back seat of my father's Gremlin,
grandmother assured me you'd live

long enough to set your share of fires.
All I wanted was for you to burn

me down. Somewhere nearby, two
doves stood tail to tail, made one

four-legged blur. That's how I wanted
us. Entanglement without the split.

Not a snarl of flannel in a refrigerator
twenty miles outside Woodstock.

A handprint on a wall. Loose beads
like teeth on the floor. Gun sunk

to the bottom of a lagoon. I once
believed you had a sea burial

and fastened two bricks to my chest
just to risk a second glimpse.

A lady conjured dead near M-20.
She told me I'd lose an arm

and marry the new Prime Minister
of Canada. I knew how to hit

the floor when bullets sequined
every tabletop. The moon

made me claustrophobic, but I'd
watch the Olympics naked

in a motel that never bothered to ask
my name. Where were you

if not the skeleton they discovered
in the bowels of the stadium,

or the cross-eyed man who tumbled
through a roof, into an atrium.

Nobody noticed until the rain ruined
the hundred-dollar pear soufflé.

I looked for you under the sheets
of sod my father lined along

the edges of the yard. Of course
you weren't there. The frogs

told me otherwise. Some moon
hid itself from view. Lone

girl with hair spread out in water.
A map that would become

the palm of your hand. No longer
hiding your body from mine.

A DIORAMA

I still marveled at the size of you,
though now we slept on a bed of painted
corduroy and drank from a stretch of mica.

The hawk continued to live in the air.
A mechanized moon followed our every
move. You had no hammer, but we

didn't need one. I was forever polishing
the same grain of salt. In ten years
we'd received bonnets. A team of horses

for you and a rifle for me, after canning
the summer's peaches. One day
we woke to an unfamiliar backdrop,

lupine and sedge painted in the distance.
Maybe some elk, but you called them
reindeer, pressing your thumb into

the flat center of my palm. My head
once broke through the bedroom wall:
not cardboard, but glossed paper. Nobody

anticipated our vigor. We made tinder
into a raging conflagration, only in small
scale. It took weeks for them to identify

the source of purple streaks on my neck,
variety of the burn on your tailbone.
It wasn't from fire. Everything still fit.

The night janitor was the first to notice
the bundle in my basket wasn't plums.
We'd anticipated the arrival, hung

extra cellophane over all windows.
Soon people were sacrificing two times
the admission just to touch our glass.

I kept the baby quiet on my tiny breast
(which was surprisingly malleable).
Women left candles and wept.

One day I strapped him to your chest
with a frill of blue elastic from stray
underpants. *A second coming*, they said.

The mechanical moon burned out
and nobody bothered to fix the gears.
We readied ourselves for a hard winter:

three pioneers keeping warm before
a battery-powered fire, the country
around us oblivious with snow.

DISTURBANCE NEAR AN UNNAMED CREEK

We both took turns holding me down.
They had outlined the woods with orange
flags, tongue depressors scattered in grass.
We were all the minuscule bones of the ear
except one. I was a basket of eggs the night
before a tornado, contents already unsteady
as if they knew what was coming. You were,
and then for several moments the creek stood
half-quiet. If there was ever something worth
starving for, I couldn't name it. My theories
too tympanic to support their own existence.

At this point in the story we were destined
to find a ramshackle cottage built into a cliff.
A blue water glass on what posed as a counter
but was really a coffin, an old steamer trunk.
The back of a horse that once carried its rider
through a controlled burn, and lived to pass
flames from roof to roof. No reason for us to
spend the night on a rope bed long abandoned.
The creek ran clear through the living room.
It made a slow creep up the stairway, perhaps
magnetic, the way things happen in Michigan.
You smashed the glass window, then I did.
Put your ear to the ground like a true expert,
my cheekbone to the ground like a clay pot
stripped of its finish, sent back to its genesis.

A PETRIFIED FOREST

We contemplated our badlands.
The villagers kept blessing us,
but then they wanted our blessing.

At the moment I was supposed to
fling myself into your arms, running
the length of a football field in heels,

a man blustered in with his dog.
Everything was off-kilter, or demotic.
The squirrels were all mechanical,

or so they told us. Why not just throw
knives at the sky? Why not a toast
to the world's oldest bacterium, now

trussed like a goose and available
for less than a timeshare in Canada?
The ruckus downstream was the terror

I felt when a banana sang to me
on my seventh birthday. Something
between a slipped disc and a mouth

full of chalk dust. We both endured
a tour with a guide, volcanic activity
and petrifaction, and all I could say

despite the sequined fanny packs
around me was *you call that hard?*
I had something far more seaworthy

in my hand. We hid under a leaf pile.
Sure, it was juvenile. But you were
a live oak, and I was no naturalist.

GEM OF THE NORTH

They say that the earth is the devil's
handkerchief, white beaches of Beulah,

Michigan the ashtray of a thousand saints.
But I had never been there. Did not pry

open the locked cabinet of the shanty
they rented us weekly. It must've been

some other city. You never licked my
ankle in the dim corners of Point Betsie

Lighthouse. There were no corners,
anyway. Had we stopped in Beulah,

we could've witnessed the most dull
bridge in history, perused the ample

documentation that won it the title.
I'd name Beulah after the last man

shot in the first battle. Of the .4 miles
that make up Beulah, none are charted

underwater, leaving the other .2 for us.
And how to occupy them best? Start

with unyielding cruise control, two
blueberry donuts without filling.

Do not drink water from the taps.
The toilets in Beulah flow upward,

not down to the sewer, but to the sky,
all the trailer hitches gleaming like sins.

A REDACTION

They made honey illegal. Decreed white paint
illicit, baby, so let's invent rollers out of shirts
and blank this out for good. Save a room next

door for the buttons we won't ever need again.
I broke the law of threes. There was no three.
Why keep pretending just to make hands safer.

It was create your own threat day. It was sell
what you don't have day, but in a neighboring
county where all walls were painted eggshell.

I kept wondering how hard our iron headboard
would have to slam to crack the walls, my head
tilted in a way that recalled Klimt, or terrorism.

The transcriptionist looked like she was noting
everything, but really she was pushing her keys
in imitation of a harpsichord. How it reminded

her of alchemy, of a fence she painted in honey.
So baby, when tonight we set out on foot, only
a stainless steel sauce pan to our name, bereft

of the sort of dog that always saves, lacking all
sense of making fire, please recall this precise
moment. I used to work in a building that lit up

in flame every afternoon, in the winter. Even
then I knew I loved you. I could have thrown
myself into the Thames, shirt bloated with red

embers, mouth full of poison, a back rippling
with arrows, the lances through my hands, or
rope around the whole lot. Instead, I waited.

COMMITTEE OF THE WHOLE

When you said you wanted to sleep
under my sticks, did you mean a body

or a house? We disregarded the motion
on the floor. Likely another nut dropped

from the buckeye outside my window.
Sometimes the bullet landed precisely

in the mouth of a passerby. At our best
we were medicinal. All of our business

was new business, our questions fringed
like the trembling grass cusp of a ravine.

At our worst we were not parliamentary.
We took turns being the one on the table.

Was that *amen* you were saying? Or only
the shutters readying themselves for rain,

children streaming indoors from mines
they dug into the hillside. No, you said

amend. The alleluia was just imaginary,
the quorum of your pockets spread out

across my windowsill as after a tornado.
It was far too soon to call the question.

A TRICK KNEE

My humor was not an ill humor.
The cables holding my bones to other
bones were most forgivable.

It's not possible to sink
into yourself like my car keys
into the swamp where I threw them.

The bones you rode in on.
The bones that rode you back home.
The secret is to keep moving

like you mean it. Peer over
your shoulder and a roof collapses
under the weight of its squirrels.

A collective bargain. You cut your
finger and I'll bleed mine.
The diagnosis: perfect health,

if not a hint of the remarkable.
Those cement blocks aren't heavy
after all. I'll save one for your

back. We'll move them downstream
to where there's no circulation.
Nothing left in the world to get down on.

AN EXCURSION

I wrote your name backwards
on my hand until it hurt.

You dropped a cube of cheese
into the crystal punch bowl.

At first we didn't realize these
activities were connected.

The only way to cleanse a hand
is through something bright

red and seething. I defined for
you: seething. It's a mouth

where a mouth should never be.
In that way my neck owes

its sun and moon to the table
that shielded us. Not so

vulnerable at the first instance
of thunder, comparatively.

Some nights we just slammed
ourselves against all doors

in the hotel, screaming *our love
is better than your love.*

Nothing could be more true,
even if those polyester

desk clerks made us scrub all
our sticky ellipses off

the linoleum. We were not shy
at the continental breakfast

the next day, overflowing soda
glasses and heaping eggs

onto each other's plates. Who
was that whispering into

the hot sauce, complaining
about the broken ice

machine? And how we took
the whole thing out

with one slam from my back?
The cubes had no desire

for marginalia anyway, so it
should be a contribution.

Thank goodness the elevator
had been inspected yearly.

A PROCLAMATION

I say the word, and nothing happens.
I say to you, in the darkest of caverns,
the only surviving light green light

stored in a tin can until punctured,
the willow trees so indecipherable
with tangles, hallelujah, above us.

The only existing copy of the treatise
was hung for comic effect, burned,
burned again when some edges kept

like daisies to mock the dignitaries.
We met under the great spectacle
in the year of the great spectacle.

Nobody could have orchestrated it
better. Sometimes you just have to
let a planet rub against its neighbor.

Sometimes a pocket is not meant
for explosives. I ignored the theory
of hand-to-ammunition diplomacy.

It took all of my mettle to ask you.
My mettle was composed of twelve
ounces of vodka and one shipwreck.

My mettle escaped from an antique
prison where the bars were optional
but everyone still requested them.

In the pit of an abandoned ocean
liner, crouched in a musty bunker,
beneath the splendor of a pancake

with a hot nail through the middle,
I say the word. The flames not instant
as predicted, but raging shortly after.

A DRAPERY

The two panels never quite met
in the middle, so we laundered them

with a halved lemon and shook
the wrinkles out in the sun.

Our neighbors were burning old
shoes in a metal drum. None of this

disturbed our project. Dedication
was what made us most famous, not

the beaded tambourines we sold
at major intersections. One day

we hoped to never separate again.
To live in a house of conveyor belts

and pulleys, though we'd never touch
them. Nothing we did was for show.

I'd never forget the outline of your
face. Even if houses collapsed, forest

growing through the floor in days.
Everything with us had a certain

permanence the rest of the world
lacked. The only place for me

was poured across your body.
Not like a cement mixer backs its

goods onto the walk, but like batter
inching its way along the crêpe pan,

or blood shuttling down a length
of gauze. My mouth tasted of your

favorite red candy. We vowed to
never hang those curtains up again.

A HEX SYMBOL

Now that we no longer have to drive to Pennsylvania,
I prefer my stars not to be stylized, my rosettes uncomfortably
explicit. Nobody can stop staring at them. Everyone should
strive for parity of some sort, even if long skirts don't flatter.
You always said I'd look hot in a bonnet. When I begged you
to hang the pineapple hex over our bed, you did not resist
at first. We had no barn door, aside from the metaphor, and no
horse would walk out of that one alone. Nights when we smoked
under a canopy of electrical wires and oak leaves, no talk
of moving to the country. Our neighbors burned their incense,
squeezed the rice from stuffed peppers. Our gray cat executed
her nightly rounds. There was no symbol for all of these things
transpiring in unison. I always sliced too close to the core
of the pineapple. We had to stay far away from the sun wheel
until later. My cape and apron only made me look gothic, not
married. After a while it started to drizzle. The cat intercepted
two distlefinks on their way to the thistle feeder. The feathers
made a bird of paradise on the sidewalk, a tiny sun in the gutter.

A BRAVERY

Say nothing about my bravery
that you wouldn't say into an empty

suitcase, or a grapefruit minus
its contents. Together we equaled

the weight of one average
Midwesterner. That's not to say

we were lacking. Absolutely
not. Why not just indict the sky

or accuse the clouds of failing
to hold enough nectarines to drown

an entire village. Some truths
are absolute. Example: yesterday

when I wore my diaphanous
skirt and climbed you like a grain

elevator. Wheat, gravel, corn,
it was all skin to me from the start.

They tell you death is fast,
a little scrambling. We will never

find out, will we. I write it on
the left hand of you, the man I love.

Use a potato peeler to render
every toilet in the women's room

inoperable. I learn curses
from an ancient book of garbage.

Somewhere, an anonymous
front stoop holds you like I should.

Until then, the only pies
that cool will be cooling for you.

RIP CURRENT

I could always feel my way out.
On my back in the storm sewer

counting minutes until day
left. Nobody to dig my sneakers

from sand. The way my arm
touched yours without touching.

If we had a boat I'd bail it.
In this case, only slip made

at the edge of the beach. What
cover. As if I had found you

between daylilies and machine
guns in the encyclopedia. Gold

edges I would lick as a child,
wanting them to light me up.

Strange how corrugated metal
warms. I once hid volume ten

under my mattress at night.
Next day it was burning

in the sink. I shook my head.
It was the first time I loved

my legs. Everything turned to
a blink of what it had been.

The butcher store cow cut
into geometric wallpaper.

Baguettes trembled. Knees
turned on themselves, then

on each other. Except mine.
In the center of volume ten:

a map, in color. The kind
of prayer we made with it.

ACKNOWLEDGMENTS

Grateful acknowledgment is made to the editors of the following magazines in which these poems first appeared, sometimes in slightly different versions.

Barrelhouse: Disturbance Near an Unnamed Creek
Center: A Journal of the Literary Arts: A Drapery, O Holy Insurgency
The Collagist: Portrait of Myself as a Piece of Red Candy in Your Mouth
Copper Nickel: Metropolis, Prelude to Our Escape
Diode: Heresy, My God, Route 31, Where You Store the Gun at Night
Ducts.org: Gem of the North, Simplicity Pattern #2519
Dusie: Collections, Saint Vodka
Fire on Her Tongue: The Business of It, A Coronation, An Incarnation
Gulf Coast: Craftsman
The Journal: Confabulations, Confluence, Forensics
The Minnesota Review: A Diorama
The National Poetry Review: A Poverty, A Trick Knee
North American Review: Dyes and Stitchery
The November 3rd Club: A Gauntlet
Passages North: Ode to Your Innocence
Prime: A Very Hard Time
Puerto del Sol: A Pact, Naturalism, Committee of the Whole
The Rumpus: An Excursion
South Dakota Review: A Bravery
Thermos: A Bildungsroman, A Hex Symbol
Valparaiso Poetry Review: Treaty Line
Waccamaw: A Genesis

This work would not have been possible without an Individual Excellence Award from the Ohio Arts Council.

Many thanks to the friends and colleagues who believed in me and supported this project in one way or another: Elizabeth J. Colen,

Oliver de la Paz, Thomas Dukes, Michael Dumanis, John Gallaher, David Giffels, Matthew Guenette, Carol Guess, Steve Kistulentz, Mike Krutel, Erika Meitner, Michael Meyerhofer, Aimee Nezhukumatathil, Bob Pope, Lee Ann Roripaugh, Jessica Schantz, Amy Bracken Sparks, Bill Thelin, Eric Wasserman, and Catherine Wing. Special thanks to Amy Freels, Diane Goettel, Susan Grimm, Elizabeth Tussey, and Jay Robinson. My endless gratitude to Black Lawrence Press, Dzanc Books, designer Rebecca Maslen, and cover artist David Oster. Much love and gratitude to my parents, Patsy and Scott Biddinger, and to my family: Eric, Gabi, and Ray.

Photo by Eric Morris

Mary Biddinger is the author of the poetry collections *Prairie Fever* (Steel Toe Books, 2007) and *Saint Monica* (Black Lawrence Press, 2011), and co-editor of one volume of criticism: *The Monkey and the Wrench: Essays into Contemporary Poetics* (U Akron P, 2011). She edits *Barn Owl Review*, the Akron Series in Poetry, and the Akron Series in Contemporary Poetics, and teaches literature and creative writing at the University of Akron.